Bilingual Edition

Edición bilingüe

Let's Draw a
Dinosaur with Shapes

Vamos a dibujar un
dinosaurio usando figuras

The Rosen Publishing Group's
PowerStart Press™ & **Editorial Buenas Letras**™
New York

For Joey / Para Joey

Published in 2005 by The Rosen Publishing Group, Inc.
29 East 21st Street, New York, NY 10010

First Edition

Book Design: Emily Muschinske

Photo Credits: p. 23 © Corbis/Royalty Free.

Library of Congress Cataloging-in-Publication Data

Randolph, Joanne.
Let's draw a dinosaur with shapes = Vamos a dibujar un dinosaurio usando figuras / Joanne Randolph ; translated by Mauricio Velázquez de León.
    p. cm. – (Let's draw with shapes = Vamos a dibujar usando figuras)
Includes index.
ISBN 1-4042-7553-3 (library binding)
1. Dinosaurs in art–Juvenile literature. 2. Drawing–Technique–Juvenile literature. I. Title: Vamos a dibujar un dinosaurio usando figuras. II. Title. III. Let's draw with shapes.
NC780.5.R36 2005b
743.6–dc22
                                        2004003662

Manufactured in the United States of America

Due to the changing nature of Internet links, Editorial Buenas Letras has developed an online list of Web sites related to the subject of this book. This site is updated regularly. Please use this link to access the list:
http://www.buenasletraslinks.com/ldwsh/dino

2

Contents

Contenido

Draw a red oval for the head of your dinosaur. Add a red rectangle for the neck.

Dibuja un óvalo rojo para hacer la cabeza de tu dinosaurio. Luego dibuja el cuello con un rectángulo rojo.

4

Add an orange oval for the body of your dinosaur. Draw an orange triangle for the tail.

Dibuja el cuerpo de tu dinosaurio con un óvalo anaranjado. Dibuja la cola con un triángulo anaranjado.

6

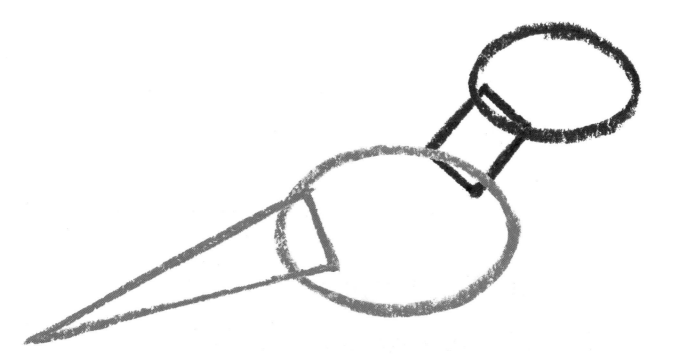

Draw two yellow rectangles for the arms of your dinosaur.

Dibuja los brazos de tu dinosaurio con dos rectángulos amarillos.

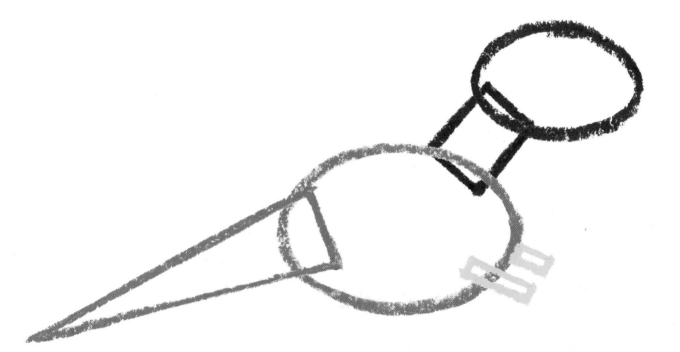

Add four green rectangles for the legs of your dinosaur.

Dibuja las piernas de tu dinosaurio con cuatro rectángulos verdes.

Draw two small blue triangles for the feet of your dinosaur.

Dibuja dos pequeños triángulos azules para hacer los pies de tu dinosaurio.

Add two purple half circles
for the hands of your
dinosaur.

Dibuja dos semicírculos
violeta para hacer las
manos de tu dinosaurio.

Draw a big pink triangle for the mouth of your dinosaur. Add six small pink triangles for teeth.

Dibuja un triángulo rosa para hacer la boca de tu dinosaurio. Dibuja sus dientes con seis pequeños triángulos de color rosa.

Add a black half circle and a small black circle for the eye of your dinosaur.

Dibuja un semicírculo y un círculo pequeño de color negro para hacer el ojo de tu dinosaurio.

19

Color in your dinosaur.

Colorea tu dinosaurio.

This dinosaur is a
Tyrannosaurus rex.

Este dinosaurio es un
Tyrannosaurus rex.